Social Media Marketing

The Ultimate Beginner's Guide to Mastery

Table of Contents

Introduction

Social media marketing has changed the marketing approach of businesses completely. Whether it is a small business, or a medium business you own, embracing social media marketing is vital for the growth and profitability of your business.

For starters, the strategy enables you to reach out to more number of customers and grab their attention via brand interaction in the various social media platforms.

A solid social media marketing strategy and web presence are two key elements needed to garner customer interest. When you do this perfectly, you can be guaranteed of a quick, effective and remarkable success in your business.

In short, SMM (Social Media Marketing) is an online marketing strategy that uses the different social media platforms such as Facebook, Twitter, Instagram etc., to accomplish branding goals and marketing communication.

The strategy involves activities such as social sharing of videos, content and images. This boosts marketing and paid advertising in social media.

This eBook is a comprehensive take on social media marketing. The techniques and tips provided will help you capitalize on the successful internet marketing strategy. You will not have to spend on SMM services or a SMM agency.

This book will help you develop your own social media marketing plan with the overview, practices and dominating tips provided.

This book will help you in several objectives such as:

- Increase traffic to your website
- Build conversions
- Raise brand awareness
- Create positive brand relationship and identity
- Improve interaction and communication with target audience
- Measure social media ROI

Social media is an easy and fun way for lead generation. You can generate leads with simple call to actions.

With paid SMM advertising, you can actually increase your benefits, as you can generate leads and expand your audience simultaneously.

From building customer relationship, distributing content to communicating with customers SMM is of tremendous help.

If you are not on Social media, you are missing out on an extensive marketing opportunity. Read this book to know how you can turn social media to your advantage easily and effectively.

Chapter 1: Are you Social media Savvy?

In the present scenario, not knowing about social media can deprive your business of a crucial marketing strategy. Social media, which includes networks such as Facebook, Google +, Twitter, YouTube, LinkedIn and Tumblr, is an enormous platform.

Social media has broken several records in being the fastest developing trend in world history. In fact, its popularity is even greater and faster than the web itself.

While the internet has managed to amass about one billion users in a decade, Facebook has in the same time managed to reach 1.49 billion users. Amazing, isn't it?

Even though the world population has grown to over 7 billion by now, 1 out of every 5 humans on this planet has a Facebook account. And this is much bigger than China, which has the biggest population worldwide.

The statistics are based on the active users on Facebook, who use it one time at least per month.

So, it does pay to be social media savvy, if you want to have a competitive edge, and cross the barriers thatthe usual conventional marketing strategies pose.

Why social media marketing?

Social media marketing, in simple words, is creating content which is customized to fit the individual social media networks for the purpose of encourage sharing and user engagement.

Social media marketing is the best and most effective way to drive traffic to your site. To reach this target, you need to have impressive content related to the specific platform you use the content for.

While everyone aims at making their content go viral with varying degrees of success, it is not possible without a proper social media marketing plan.

You need to have engaging content, which grabs attention and makes people share it with others. If this is not possible your entire strategy will be a wasted effort.

While platforms such as Facebook and Twitter are mostly talked about, there are several other platforms which are equally good. There are actually over 200 such networks, according to Wikipedia.

With so many networks to play in, the social media kingdom is developing at an amazingly fast rate. Even if you are just taking your first step, you can begin with the networks, which have been there for a long time.

So, creating an account and running it successfully on Twitter or Facebook is a surefire way to start your social media marketing venture with a bang.

Tips to a smart social media approach

To be social media savvy, you need to be familiar with some important terms used in social media.

Content:

This refers to whatever posts you make on your social media page. This can include a simple status update on Facebook or a photo on your Instagram account, an interesting tweet, or a pin on Pinterest. As you can see, content can be in different forms. What you need to be particular about is customizing it, according to the platform it goes in.

Context:
Context is even more crucial, when compared to your content. The context in which you place your content can make it a success or failure. For instance, if you place an important and attractive quote in the middle of a long blog post, the chances of the quote being noticed is very minimal.

On the other hand, if you tweet it, you can nail it just like that!

But you can't always depend on a tweet to say everything you want to. An attention grabbing call to action and relevant Hashtags to go with it would be better in impressing the visitors.

Hashtags
Hashtags, which started out in Twitter, are now part of all social media networks. The hash tags describe the topic of content and make them stand out as part of the trending content. While for a beginner these may be confusing and pointless, these are actually powerful tools to create instant user engagement and boost awareness about your brand. With a hashtag your content will be easy to discover and the chances of it being shared will be more.

Share:
Shares are highly valued in the world of social media. While potential reach, click through spped and impressions may be talked about much what matters most is whether people share your content or not. While engaging a user and interacting with the user may be considered effective, it is the shares that show your efforts have paid off big. With more number of shares your content will be popular. This is a kind of engagement that users can form with your content.

Engagement:
This is a general term that denotes people are interacting with the content you have posted. This interaction can be in the form of shares, comments or recommendations.

And besides the above social media terms, there are countless number of terms that make up the platform and play a key role in making it a successful one.

Wake up to social media
Did you know that social media is the fastest method to make your product, brand or service reach users worldwide.

A single tweet can work wonders, zooming around the world much faster than any traditional media. Social media is the latest trend that has millions spending a major part of their precious time in it. If you intend to reach out to them, this is the place to go.

Earlier billboards were thought of as good marketing strategy, as people spend a reasonable amount of time driving.

Now, people spend more time on the various social media networks, so utilizing this trend is the smart way to turn around your business into a profit churner.

And most important of all, social media is wielding a great level of influence on users as many of them become customers via Twitter, Facebook and other such platforms.

Just a few years back, social media was considered as an innovative marketing platform, but now it has become the norm. To use it to your advantage, you need to be as knowledgeable in social media, as you can.

At the outset there will be many doubts and questions in your mind regarding social media marketing such as,

How do I know which social marketing plan I need and which is irrelevant?

Do I need to have an account on all the networks? Which is the best of all?

How to manage the conversation?

Andthere are much more of such queries.

Tips for embracing social media

For beginners, using social media may seem overwhelming. Here are a few tips to guide you on the right social media marketing strategy

Decide on the most valuable network

When you start planning your SMM strategy, the best way to go about it is by eliminating the networks you want to avoid. While it has been thought erroneously that showing a presence on as much outlets as you can, would give more results, it can backfire in the most damaging way.

Since all networks are not relevant for a specific business, you need to know which platforms would serve well for your business and make it look authentic.

So, start listing the social media platforms, which are the most valuable and a list of the minimum value platforms. And contrary to popular belief in social media, less is always more.

This is because to be active on a social platform, you have to put in sufficient effort on the conversations, valuable content posting, and monitoring the response continuously. Doing this on several platforms can be tiring, and an entire waste of your time and energy.

Instead of having sparse conversations with several people, over many platforms think of valuable, personal and highly relevant conversations with a few numbers of people, on a few handful of the social media platforms. This would definitely bring value in the long term.

Be consistent

Once you narrow down the platforms and choose the most valuable ones, you should think about planning a reliable schedule for posting, which will not be interrupted in any way.

When you are not posting regularly, it doesn't make any sense to be on a platform. Here are some things to consider on managing the platforms:

- *Assign an individual to take over the time consuming and challenging task of monitoring the social media pages.*
- *Be clear on the space ownership and chart a plan on how you can be consistent in your posting in such a way that both your brand voice and postings are consistent.*
- *Being consistent is important as it helps you view prospectively the importance of an outlet. If the platform is not used for posting content relevant to your business, you should not consider being on it.*

Risks hone your social media skills

The risks involved in social media presence depend on the industry sector you are in. Taking risks should not be avoided. Risky approaches include displaying images of day to day activities in your business establishment, sharing the issues you face with your staff and so on.

Such types of risks pay off handsomely, when you take relevant and honest risks. Since users are partial to transparency and genuineness, showing them some real time snaps of the business will work out in your favor.

Chapter 2: Social Media: Best Practices for higher ROI

Very rarely do you come across a website that doesn't ask you to Follow it on Twitter or Like it in Facebook. At present, businesses have taken up to blindly following a success format without rhyme or reason. This results in just short term progress, which is not of much importance.

Many businesses concentrate on the numbers without analyzing who they want to reach and how to engage their customers. Without the presence of relevant and mature content, and proper engagement strategy, you may end up with more unlikes and unfollows.

Sharpen your perspective

The key to a successful SMM strategy is, knowing that your audience cannot be categorized into one single group. And further, you have to realize that branded messages, Tweet/win/like contests and marketing campaigns do not have a sustainable market. So, you should create a channel for your brand that has a mission, purpose and value.

There is no magical number of networks you can use to get the required exposure, engagement and sales. You need to create sufficient channels that help to strengthen the concentration of your brand, service or product.

Create channels which boost the brand message, instead of diluting it. And most importantly, you should be able to manage the channels and update them regularly and keep their relevance intact.

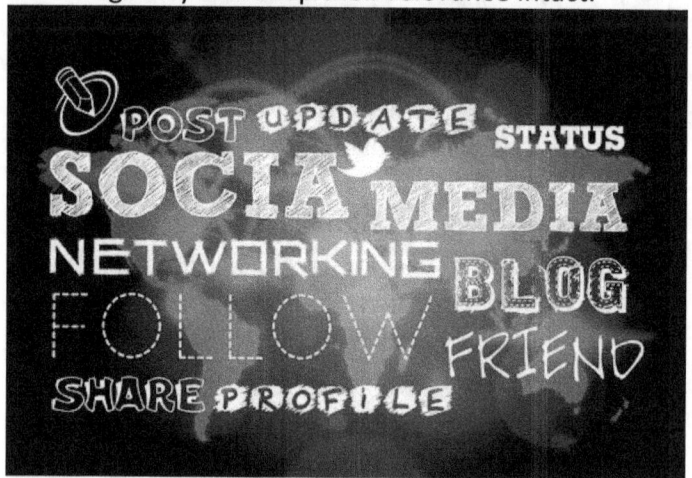

Here are some of the SMM best practices that drive social stream engagement effectively.

Create a dynamic network presence

Assess the important aspects of your sub brands, your brand and also the eminent celebrities who can influence user engagement. When you find channels that do not feature in the initial plan, analyze their worth as an independent entity and their present state. You can either truncate the accounts or close all of them.

Form a solid support system

Managing different accounts in social media needs a strong organized system to support every presence exclusively. Make sure every account meets with the audience needs appropriately.

Purpose oriented

You need to identify your target audience first. Decide and establish a communicable objective and mission for every account.

Editorial program

Each account has to cater to various requirements such as engagement, service, sales, entertainment etc. To ensure this happens accurately and right on target, you should design an editorial system. Focus on creating content which is relevant, shareable and engaging.

The KISS (Keep it Significant and Shareable) metric should be adhered to. Out of the box concepts help to bring in a fresh perspective and renewed interest. Use promotional content, polls, questions etc. to gain a competitive advantage.

Monitor the system

Build a team of monitors to assess the distinct conversations and brands in each account. This will help you to make the necessary additions or changes, and make your social media accounts fully functional.

Establish seamless workflow

Every account needs a proper format for a smooth flow of information and work activities. And the accounts need to be interconnected, so everyone involved will function seamlessly by responding or engaging, according to the situation.

Having a flow chart drawn to help representatives take decisive actions will help in a better engagement. When they know the decisions to be made in specific situations, they will be able to do it in real time.

Conduct ongoing training to keep representatives on track. Create a social group and have a reward system to make them more focused and sharp.

Draft a style guide for social media that defines your brand's voice, essence, characteristics and personality perfectly.

Design specific rules and the things to avoid, in your SMM plan. A properly created guide would be an effective path to your success.

Use effective customer engagement techniques

To serve existing and prospective customers effectively, you need to answer their queries and provide a solution for their problem. A service feature should be dedicated for every account to meet with such needs. This will promote loyalty and appreciation.

Timing of your updates and tweets decide on the entire engagement and reach, so try optimizing the timing and language of your content.

Monitoring every account's performance closely will help to improve the strategies already in place.

Consider cross promotion

Although it may seem counterproductive and even detrimental to your brand, cross promotion actually helps a great deal. The reason is very simple. With the extensive reach of the social networks and the innumerable brands present, not to mention the huge network of people frequenting the networks, there is very little chance of such an approach failing. But make sure you do not post in a wrong format or blindly.

And while you are at it, consider promoting other content too. But, ensure the ratio is properly met with. Your account should have a decent blend of information, in addition to brand centric content. The priority should be on relevance and value in the content.

Genuineness pays

Your social media page should be a reflection of your brand, service or product. The users would prefer looking at the true personality of your business service and not a disconnected version.

Make sure the content is pleasant enough to make the audience evince interest. They would react positively by starting an interaction and then share the content.

And, when mistakes happen, do not panic. The lessons you learn, although by the hard way, will be very valuable. Whether your content does not get any engagement, or the audience hates your content, you will know the things to shun away from.

Since social media is still in its fledgling stage, it is not possible to have hard and fast rules to succeed in it. So forge ahead, learn from your mistakes and whenever possible get guidance from the experts. The best practices mentioned above will strengthen your brand and prevent it from being engulfed by customer unfollows and unlikes. When you focus on the social networks and pay diligent attention to each, you can certainly improve customer experience and have a higher engagement.

Meaningful interactions will boost your brand's reach dramatically, and customers will not just like it, but truly love your brand.

Chapter 3: Tips On How To Dominate Facebook

Founded by Mark Zuckerberg and his fellow students at Harvard in 2004, Facebook had become a phenomenon that has broken many records in terms of followers, brand marketing and sales.

Initially available to only Harvard students, the network expanded to Ivy League and now it is the largest ever social network.

By having your ads on Facebook, you can target your specific customers effectively and reach a spectacular conversion rate.

Content freedom

The videos, text posts and images in Facebook allow you complete freedom to optimize your content and make it viral. As long as you integrate your content as much as you can, it will be a win all situation for you.

You can load your YouTube videos on your Facebook page, instead of a link to the video. You can add tabs to your landing page or giveaway in the fan page. The longer you keep visitors on your page, the better will be your success rate, as people have trust in the platform and would not wish to leave it.

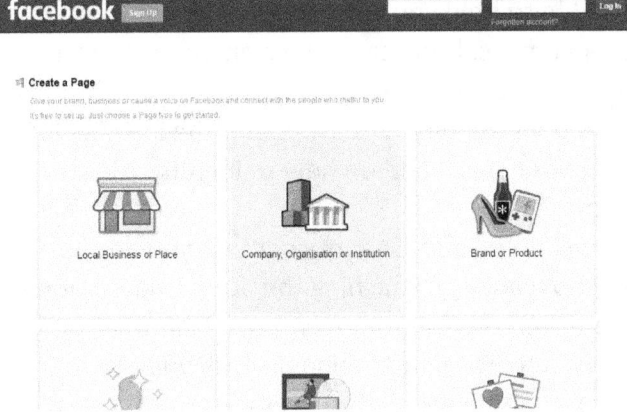

Maximum reach

To dominate on Facebook, you don't just need likes but a wider reach. Reach helps to measure your success in social media marketing far better than the likes you get. With increased reach, conversions can be increased.

Use dark posts

Dark posts are very effective in reaching out to your target audience. These posts let you post on your page without being visible in your general feed. You can target fresh communities and users who have not yet liked your page. The posts are easy to publish. You can tweak them and check their impact to know about the extent of their success.

Facebook ads

Facebook has immense amount of data that can be exploited in a multitude of ways. With Facebook ads, you can make deeper inroads into your marketing than ever before.

Make use of the easy instruction guides and tutorials available to help you with posting the ads. A mere $20 ad on Facebook can have tremendous reach.

Have an eye on audience insights

Located on top of your dashboard, the insights teach about your reach and on how to identify your customers.

This will help you assess the content you are posting and know about it reaching the appropriate people. Whenever you test your new posts, this area will show changes or fluctuations, which you can interpret and apply with success.

Reevaluate your organic posts

Since Facebook has changed in to a pay for service network, you should assess on the money you have to spend on each content segment.

The time taken and the number of people reached with a single piece,pinpoint the effectiveness of the post.

For instance, if you get 6 views and receive 12k from 4 clients, and you have used 6k for the ads, the number of views is reasonably good ROI. But you should consider this in specific relation to your business.

Chapter 4: Tips on How to dominate Instagram

Instagram tasted success right off from its first step. The app was perfect in all aspects. Within a space of 3 months, the app had reached over 1 million users. And in a single year, Facebook acquired it for an amazing amount of 1 billion dollars in 2012. Now it has over 400 million users in its fifth year.

Recently Instagram has released ads for use by all. Instagram is purely about pictures and this may be the reason it has the most engagement rate.

The site is easy to post your likes. You just have to double tap on a picture, in contrast to what you do on Facebook or Twitter.

Although videos are present, they are not as big a hit as the pictures. But interesting and short videos of duration as low as 15 seconds, do work well here. But you need to use features such as call to action, hashtags and ensure you have your bio properly done, to make SMM a hit on this network.

Here are some tips to help you

• Reveal what goes on behind the screen to ensure you strengthen the bond with your followers. Knowing what happens inside your business will give a sense of brand intimacy with the users, which creates more conversion rates

• Contests are best for interaction. They will help the customers relate to the brand and build a solid connection. This will increase your followers

• While pictures of your service or product work well, you also need to include some fun element. Add fun posts as often as you can to increase interest

• Create a simple profile. Ensure your image and profile is linked to your brand

• Avoid saturating the feed of your followers with your posts. This can cause them to unfollow you

• Choose filters, which are related to your brand image and theme

• If you have pictures of customers using your brand or product post it.

• Make sure you post good, appealing and interesting pictures and videos. Ensure your posts cast your business in the right light

Chapter 5: Tips on How to Dominate Twitter

Increasing awareness of your small or medium scale business with social media marketing may seem an uphill task at the outset. But this is not true.

Your followers and fans create an avalanche like effect. Once you toil enough to get a few followers with your retweets, it is possible to make them increase exponentially. Being patient will reap you rich rewards. Going viral is not an overnight phenomenon.

You can grow your brand with Twitter without spending much time or using a separate manager for social media. Just a few minutes in a day are sufficient. Here are some tips to help you dominate Twitter.

Know Twitter

If you are not familiar with the platform it would be best, if you spend some time learning it. This will make it easier later. There are guides from popular blogs such as Moz, Mashable, CopyBlogger and many others, which you can use to know more about Twitter. Once you know the about the basics of the platform and have a profile page, you can easily accomplish winning over Twitter fans.

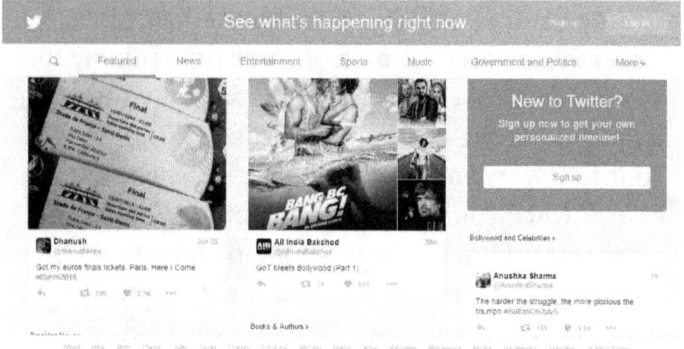

Profile set up

The bio is a key part of your Twitter account. This should be attractive and interesting. Some of the things that can accomplish this are:

•	Give an accurate detail of whom and what you are

•	Create an excitement and inspiration.

•	Associate with a perfect niche that you are genuinely part of. This will make you look authentic.

•	Be precise on your accomplishments and avoid bragging about them overtly

•	Make your lifestyle look interesting, so people will follow you.

•	Make sure you use another handle and hashtags in your bio. These will help in linking to your brand or service

Daily activity

Initially try posting regularly. Avoid any breaks for a minimum of one month. This will give the boost needed for your Twitter success.

You will get noticed this way, so do not let up. Keep focusing on improving your posts. Soon you will have followers and better traction. When you take this initial step, you will find it easier as you move on.

Follow people

By following a minimum of two people daily, you will

• Keep up your level of activity in your Twitter account. You will gain a systematic exposure

• Align yourself with the niche that is right for you. When you define your brand perfectly, it will help you use Twitter the best way. Just follow people present within your specific niche.

But when you follow too many, it can backfire. This will cause a big difference between your followers and those you follow.

Too little followers with too many people whom you follow can make you look frantic. So, following one or two people at the beginning is a safe thing to do. Once you gain more presence, your followers will definitely be more than the people you are following.

People to follow

Choose the people to follow from the Twitter list of people you might have interest in. If you do not find anyone interesting, click on the refresh tab and look at a new group of people.

You should know about the popular names and celebrities in your niche. Following such people will help you have new insights on your business. You can also network their followers.

Following the people who are followed by the leaders in your field is a good tactic. To find about these people, view the profile of the industry leaders and find their followers by clicking on the Following tab. Now you have a list of people you can follow

Activities to adhere to

Discover a few top items related to your niche in the Discover tab of Twitter and retweet them.

Monitor your notifications and keep track of things. This will keep you in the loop and let you be part of the excitement and buzz.

Follow your followers back, provided they are not a very huge number. At the beginning, when you have a few followers this will work better

When your see retweets, click on the star in the tweet. This will show your appreciation. This retweet favorite feature will increase exposure and keep you under people's eye. Also favorite all the replies you have received. Or, at least try to conclude a conversation using a favorite tab.

Tweet rules

One way to effectively tweet is to write them beforehand. Services like Hootsuite or Buffer help in this. Even if you use such sites, you should try to actively engage on your Twitter page, once in a day to keep track of trending topics.

Use a minimum of two hashtags.

When you tweet about the trending topics, which you can find on the Twitter menu, you can gain more visibility.

Tweet about the trends related to your niche. If you cannot find one, try to tweak the trend to suit your niche.

Customize the trends with the help of Twitter features, so you can focus on the topics that are in your niche. This is easy to do.

Click on the Change tab near Trends box. You will be taken through a step by step customization of tweets based on the follow list and location you are from. Customized trends help to find the most popular topics related to your field.

And finally, make sure personal branding and other content you have are in line with the activities on your Twitter account.

Chapter 6: Tips on How to Dominate LinkedIn

LinkedIn, in spite of having entered social media before Facebook, has not had a huge growth. Its success has been more of a slow and steady way. After 14 years, it has grown to more than 400 million users.

To reach its present success, the platform focused on the things that were working well like the homepage. It increased signups by about 40 percent and later increased to nearly 50 percent. Email invitations increased from 4 percent to 7 percent ,but in a much longer time.

The premium subscriptions, freemium options and paid career board were also instrumental for the platform's success during its initial years.

The features like importing contacts, professional members mostly from San Francisco technology field and integration with Pulse and SlideShare have made the platform a very profitable one.

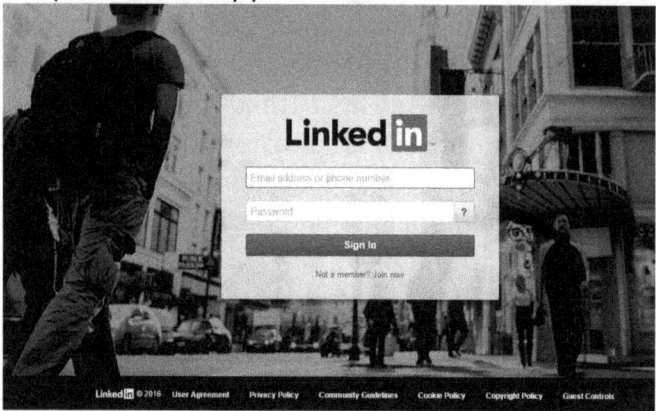

Professional focus

The platform is purely about business. You can learn anything and everything about your industry. A Slideshare on easy recipes would not fare well as a tech topic would.

The platform gives the necessary assistance to people, so they can improve their business. If you need this, LinkedIn is a good choice. It has over 102 million members worldwide, so you can benefit more, if you do some optimization.

Ranking in Search Engines

To reach the top of LinkedIn search results, you should focus on keyword placement and density. Here are the areas you should focus on:

• Headline: This attracts visitors first. So include the keywords here.

- Past and present Work Experience: This is the next important place to have your keywords
- Summary: You should use the summary to show your talent and strength. So, instead of keyword stuffing, try to include them minimally.

Ranking for keywords

The more number of keywords in your profile, the better will be your ranking. Make sure you write a job description that includes as many things that you accomplish in that job. Make it unique and keyword rich, to get top ranking.

Optimize your profile

You need to focus on three important things to optimize the profile.

Customize url: With a customized url, people will find it easy to find you. Click on edit profile feature, and in the public profile area, go to customize option and do the necessary tweaking.

Add Twitter account

Set up a Twitter page, if you don't have one. You can install Twitter by either having the tweets auto posted to the LinkedIn status, or select the tweets that have hashtag in them.

Link website with your anchor text

The links in your profile can be added to any type of anchor text. The links will count for your Google ranking. So, try to add keywords in anchor text, which you are trying to get a rank for in the search engine.

Since, more number of businesses has started using the platform for finding their new employees, you can use this platform effectively. You can be hired on a lucrative job or just be part of the professional set up to gain recognition.

Chapter 7: Tips on How to Dominate Google+

In spite of having been in the social media circle for just about five years, Google+ has amassed over 250 million users. Google + is Google's answer to Facebook. Even if Facebook is still the leader of the pack, Google+ has made considerable inroads.

Of the 2.5 billion people using Gmail, 250 million people have an activated Google+ account. But so far just 25 million have posted here and of them only about 6 million are genuinely active.

The main draw here is Google+ is integrated with Gmail. The circles concept, which Google+ uses to group all things, has made this possible. Whenever you add a person you know to the platform, you can mark them into categories such as colleague, friend or family.

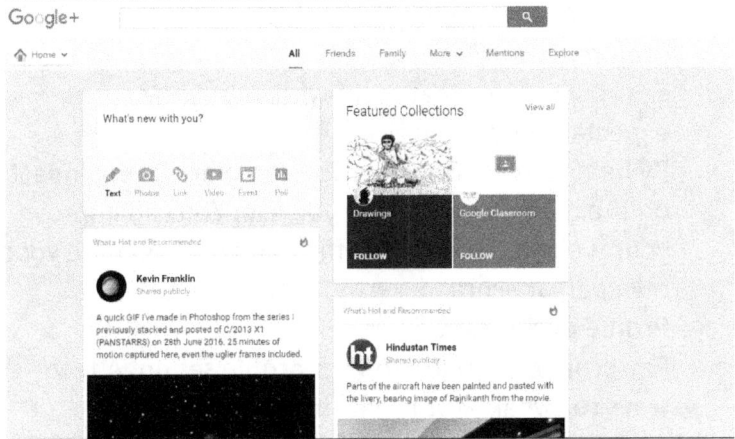

Other features that have made this platform popular include Google Hangouts, which is used for hosting webinars mostly, and the facility to add contacts directly from the notification email you have.

Perspective

You can have images, polls and videos here as in Facebook. And you can cross post here even if you have another main social platform you are active in like Facebook or Twitter. This is more so if the circles have different members than the fans in your other networks.

Why Google+

Even if you use Facebook as your primary social media marketing tool, having a strong presence in Google+ will actually increase your exposure exponentially.

For one, Google+ is affiliated to the largest and powerful ever search engine, so being on it is a definite plus for you. There are other factors too.

- A community of people with high influence

- A platform that is finely tuned to user preferences
- Features that meet with your SMM expectations and more

By being part of Google+, you can make deep impact on the marketing strategy you use. You can improve your website, increase traffic to it and dominate your own personal brand.

Profile optimization

Pay proper attention to your profile set up. A few ways to tweak your profile include

- Your summary should have info about your business and you, including your hobbies and passion. Personal info will help in conversations, when you share tidbits on your personal life.
- Make sure your profile image is of high quality and very professional
- Use the relevant keywords. Use keywords related to your industry, city, state and country. Your customers will find you easily.

Content magic

Content is the key factor to focus on in social media marketing strategy. Google+ lets you share your experience and help you become an authority in your field. With excellent content, you can boost your Google+ presence spectacularly.

Refine your contacts

With Google+ circles, you can organize your contacts based on your interests. Filtering circles helps to target your specific audience and avoid the general conversation clutter that is common in social platforms.

Join communities which are specific to your forte

Be part of a community that is related to your field, hobby or passion. You can share the best practices and improve your social media strategy

Keep tab on the Ripples

Ripples feature on Google+ lets you know about who shares your content and how popular it is. You can click the Ripples feature from the menu in your post, to measure your content's popularity. Make personal connection with everyone who shares your content. When you do this, you show that you value them. This further increases your reach.

Share images

Images form a key aspect of optimizing content. So, have appealing images including your profile photo.

Be part of Google+ Hangouts

This is a hangout similar to Skype. It is free, engaging and fun to use. You can converse with your customers, share features about your product or brand, and increase your customer base.

Google Plus Badge

The badge from Google+ developer platform, which you can display in your website profile, posts and in your community by creating a custom code will help increase your customers.

Chapter 8: Tips on How to Dominate YouTube

YouTube has had a phenomenal growth in the past decade. It has over one billion users per month. It is easy, fast to stream, free and you get instant comments on your videos. Each month over 200 million hours of YouTube videos are being watched. It has singlehandedly created and established thousands of industries and careers.   Video games became a money churning field because of this platform. You can teach things, do funny pranks, share your fitness secrets, and do about anything and everything on YouTube.

To boost your social media marketing, useyour other social media platforms to increase followers on YouTube. Give snippets, excerpts and previews of your business videos. Teasers spark curiosity and increase exposure.

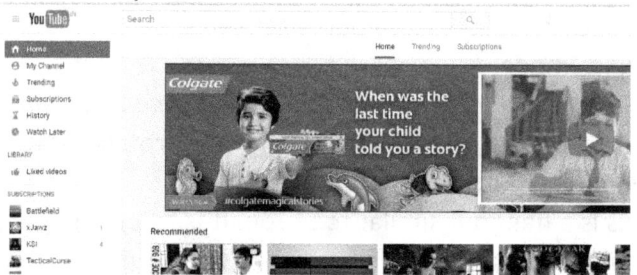

YouTube perspective

You can either teach, or entertain via YouTube, to succeed in it. You can publish videos of any length here. But make sure the content you post is consistent throughout all the social channels. Make sure you have high quality editing and recording to get your videos noticed effectively.

With Google shifting its algorithms in favor of videos, taking advantage of this platform will certainly help expand your business successfully.

Dominate YouTube tips
Video content

• Short is sweet. Short videos have more chances of being seen fully. So, try to be as concise as you can.

• Make sure the lighting is the finest to create vibrant and quality videos.

• Edit videos before you publish them. Add the best shots, cut out the pauses to get a flawless video. Make use of free editing software such as VirtualDub, iMovie and MovieMaker.

• Keyword research: Keywords are important in your videos too. Use keyword tool of YouTube to create phrases and words you want to target.

• Description link: A link in the description part will guide people watching the video to your site unerringly. Make sure the link is added right at the beginning, as the content is shown only up to 27 characters.The rest is hidden and can be revealed only by clicking on the option, 'show more'.

• And include keywords in the description. This will further boost your video's SEO.

• Video title: When you choose keywords, ensure they are in the title. If you can include the words twice, the ranking will be even better. The title should induce curiosity, promise a solution or explain why a visitor should watch it. Create a title that would make the video watched instantly.

- Use a good Call to Action asking viewers to share, like, add, comment or follow. This will increase the effect remarkably.

Video branding

Since people rarely watch the channel's name ingrained in a video, it is vital to speak about your brand in your video itself. Have your logo appear at the beginning and end, along with the tagline. An animated logo and jingle would look even better

Music

Background music makes the video more interesting, professional and fun to watch. You can get a track of your choice form the music archives available free online.

Thumbnail

You can place the video thumbnail in one of the three places namely at ¼th, ½th and ¾th mark. Use an image that is appealing and induces people to click on it.

Playlists

Playlists feature helps you to group together all your videos in a specific sequence, so they play continuously. If you have made a video series, this will help in grabbing viewer attention and increase views.

Further, the playlists are shown separately in searches, so you can rank better in the search results. Use the Playlists feature under Video Manager to create your own playlist.

Promote via other platforms

Use other social channels such as Facebook to promote your video. This would increase the popularity of the videos to a great extent.

Like with any other channel or website, it is absolutely necessary to update your YouTube page on a regular basis. Upload new videos every week or month and adhere to this schedule.

Viewers respond to the queries in your comment section, send further materials for videos and even make a video in response to yours. Encourage such activities to gain a big level of success in this platform.

Chapter 9: Tips on How to Dominate Pinterest

Pinterest is an ideal platform, if you want to target your female customers. Nearly 85 percent of the 100 million Pinterest users are women. It is a sort of huge scrapbook in digital form. While earlier an invitation was required to become a member here, it is now open to all. It is one among the top 10 of the most influential social media platforms present now.

Pinterest perspective

The trending topics here include interior design, clothing, cooking and decorations. The pin boards'position makes your pictures look good only vertically. So, you need special formatting, for your pictures to look great here.

The site is a veritable gold mine for businesses. You can connect with your prospective customers and make sales effectively via this platform.

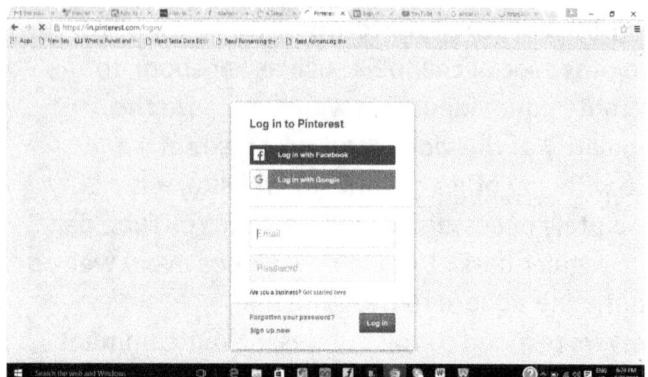

Dominating tips

When you post content, which is spectacularly useful it does really well in this platform. Useful content helps solve problems and helps you reach your goals. Since everyone is looking for useful information, which is the main reason for internet flourishing so well, providing it in an effective way either in an amusing or factual manner will have a successful reach.

With Pinterest, when you pin useful information, you get several more repins, followers and visitors. And this leads to more sales and profits.

Virtual Storefront

Pinterest enables you to create a perfect image of your brand, while other platforms like Twitter and Facebook lend it the right voice.

Likes do not matter much

Unlike Facebook, likes are not given much importance in Pinterest. Likes here are just a type of acknowledgement, but they do not endorse a pin. Repins are the main objective here.

Repins

To draw more repins, you need to focus on creating amazing content. For instance, if you are displaying flowers, ensure the images focus on the flowers. Add relevant description with keywords. This is sufficient to invite more repins.

Mobile responsive

As a majority of Pinterest traffic is from mobile gadgets, you should ensure your images are vertical and make best use of the mobile screen space. Avoid block descriptions. Make them crisp and short.

Consistent pins

Pinterest followers value regular pins. By posting regularly, but with relevant content, you can attract more viewers. Posting at the right time and in a colorful manner, while adhering to popular categories, will make your strategy a big hit here.

Contests

To make your content popular contests are vital. The contests here are of longer span, when compared to other networks. The contests should have a solid plan and follow the rules Pinterest has laid down. This will attract just the quality pins and increase your brand's awareness and reach.

While the other social networks do offer a good platform for marketing, Pinterest is emerging as a significant place for marketers. Making use of this platform therefore will add a new dimension to your marketing plan.

Chapter 10: Don't Make These Mistakes If You Want To Dominate Social Media

Businesses usually approach social media in a flippant manner. They consider it just as loading a post and seeing profit. But this is a blind approach and one that can damage your brand name and hurt your profits.

When you make haste in creating a social media marketing strategy, you are setting yourself for a massive failure. But when you follow a smart, insightful and proactive social media plan, most of the pitfalls in social media marketing can be sidestepped.

Here are some important mistakes to avoid, if you want to dominate social media and pile up profits

Underestimating social media potential

Making your social media presence popular is not an overnight task. Even if a tweet or status update is as short as 140 characters in length, every character should come together to form a coherent meaning. And your duty doesn't end with posting. You need to respond to all the negative and positive responses. Social media cannot be managed as you do a 9 to 5 regular job. You need to be on it 24/7.

This is tedious, but important work. You need to take care of creating content and monitoring it. You should hire an expert in house or find a social media management outsourcing firm.

Not identifying your target audience
Unfair and off the mark assumptions about the needs of your target audience is a common and most damaging mistake you can do to your business. Research your audience, find their preferences, and unique wishes, before you invest in your social media marketing plan.

Failing to take your competition's measure
With social media, the entire world is a playing ground. So, you should avoid seeing your competition in terms of the local businesses alone. You will be competing against world players in your field, which makes your work bigger.Although you may not be a competition to the big players, you will still beon the same bandwidth.

Not providing sufficient value
 Since the main objective of social media marketing is to build your brand, you should be careful about how often you post messages on your brand's value. This will definitely affect the quality of the content you post.

Insufficient content and more social networks
When you are starting, make sure you do not take up more than you can handle. Begin with two or three networks, which you feel will build your brand the best. Consistency is the core value to be adhered to here and not the number of social networks you are in.

Social media marketing is a skill to be perfected. You need to see to certain basics, before you plunge into the field. This will avoid many of the mistakes people make with their social media presence. Have a precise proactive plan and execute it with care targeting the right audience in a consistent manner with real value content. This will surely lead you to success.

Chapter 11: Social Media Adapt or Die

A business that has a successful social media marketing plan will be rewarded with healthier profits, when compared to a company that shies away from utilizing social media fully. In the present scenario, companies may well perish, if they do not make use of this marketing tool. Here are a few reasons as to why social media can influence your company's future.

Social media information is sacred

When you use social media analytics to tweak your social media marketing efforts, you can gain a tremendous advantage over you competitors both in the short and long term. If you fail to do this, your competitors will do so and can usurp your standing in a striking way.

Precision tactics pay big

Accuracy in doing research and implementing social media plan will become the standard for all online marketing practices. Social media information will give you an exact idea of the tastes of your customer, their social preferences and the things they like most. This can be utilized in the best possible way.

The Tailored Audience tool in Twitter is one such tool, where you can optimize a campaign, so it is seen only by the customers you specify. Without the right tactic, any money you spend on marketing will be a big drain, and result in your downfall.

New actions for new trends

With social media marketing tools, it is an entirely different ball game. You can learn more about your target customer without having to disturb them to get the information. The old standards of assessing success of marketing efforts no longer hold true here.

Social media marketing can give you accurate information on the successful strategies and the failures. You can tweak your campaign and increase its success rates. When you train your staff on how to understand social media information and use it properly, you can reap huge profits.

In short, social media marketing can become the foundation for all marketing campaigns turning them into success easily and effectively. With social media, you can connect with your audience and if you don't, you can alter it so it performs well in real time.

And best of all social media marketing helps you to know your competitors. You can even target their audience with your campaigns, when you use social media marketing effectively.

Conclusion
Social media has altered the business landscape completely in the way they use marketing tactics and how they engage their potential customers. With buyers looking to the web for solutions, having an effective social media standing has become vital.
In spite of social media being a new phenomenon, it has caused a big revolution forcing business to sit up and take notice of it. Either they make use of the social media or perish. The millions of users, social media such as Facebook show are incredible. Not having profiles in LinkedIn, Twitter, Facebook, Pinterest and others would be a strategic blunder no business would dare to commit.
Here are a few quick facts that will make this clear:
•	By spending as few as six hours in a week 64 percent marketers experienced lead generation success by using social media
•	75 percent businesses reveal an increase in traffic is the key benefit social media has given
•	89 percent of businesses using social media channels have reported a marked increase in exposure
•	Businesses using social media marketing for more than 3 years have seen a good sales increase

As you can see, social media is vital for all the businesses that are looking to create a buzz around their product or service or brand. By knowing how to dominate in the various social media platforms, you can become an undisputable leader in your field. With the guidance provided by this eBook, you can embark on your social media marketing with confidence and set your campaigns rolling and ruling the market. In spite of the tough competition out there, you have still millions of prospective people lying in wait to be touched.

Do not let your competition defeat you in the social segment. You can turn your business into a rousing success easily by embracing and dominating social media.

All the best!